the west
australian poems 1989–2009

Presenting major new work and poems selected from John Mateer's five previous Australian collections, *The West* enables readers, for the first time, to experience the range, development and cumulative power of this important Australian poet.

Grouped by affinity rather than order of publication, the poems reveal a restless subjectivity, visiting and revisiting faultlines and cultural silencings. Accepted as a poet of international significance, John Mateer is also a poet who, in the words of the critic Martin Harrison, 'speaks towards the centre of Australian culture.'

the west

australian poems 1989–2009

john mateer

🏛 FREMANTLE PRESS

John Mateer has published books of poems in Australia, as well as booklets that have appeared in Australia, South Africa, Sumatra, Japan, Macau and Portugal. Mateer's previous Fremantle Press publications are five volumes of poems, including *Barefoot Speech* which won the 2001 Victorian Premier's prize for poetry, and *Semar's Cave*, a prose travelogue on Indonesia. *Ex-white*, a collection of two decades of his South African work, was published last year in Austria, and *Namban*, a collection on vestiges of Portuguese empire, is forthcoming in Portugal. Mateer is a recipient of the Centenary Medal for his contribution to Australian literature. Born in South Africa, he spent his childhood in South Africa and Canada and, since 1989, he has lived in Australia.

... one need not notice walls, so huge is the sky.
—Randolph Stow

CONTENTS

the nature

mokare's ear

invisible cities

nothing but a foreign breeze...

Depictions of and references to deceased Aboriginal people can be distressing and offensive within Indigenous communities. Indigenous readers are therefore advised to take appropriate precautions with regard to pages 83 to 106 in this book.

The West is the Australian selection of John Mateer's poetry. It seems to me there could be a world selection of it, a South African selection, a Lisbon–Berlin reading of it and even a quite different selection based on poems written from and about various parts of South-East Asia. This is because, while Mateer has been based predominantly in Perth, he has in fact been producing parallel bodies of work from all the just mentioned places. Looked at in total, his poetry so far—individual volumes, chapbooks, sequences, translation projects, scattered publications here and overseas—is its own organisation of networks, of overlapping centres of interest. Mateer is not quite like one of his heroes, the Portuguese poet Fernando Pessoa, who wrote and published under several discrete identities; he is not heteronymous, he is not playing an identity game; but, that said, he is a poet of more than just different aspects. He is a poet of multiple projects. His work is a compilation of dividing and intersecting trajectories, often trajectories with a fair degree of independence from each other.

Australian poetry has known other poets who have set up parallel tracks, but usually this is in relation to what at the time has appeared to be the main local line: I am thinking, for instance, of permanent exiles like Randolph Stow and brilliant London-based cosmopolites like Peter Porter. Mateer, however, is a rare and novel object working directly in our midst, based here defiantly and definitely: as this book demonstrates, he is a poet who speaks towards the centre of Australian culture. Yet at the same time he is, in a quite practical way, an internationalist, based in Medan, in Kyoto, in Lisbon or Berlin. Often his work resists being localised within the familiar themes of Australian poetry—he's too South African, too Japanese, too much to do with Europe. Indeed, Mateer is hard to fix, hard to pin down. For all that, *The West* is the Australian book.

No doubt, Mateer's choice of title word 'West' references Western Australia, the place which many of these poems grow from and capture, whether in supermarkets or the highway or by the Swan River or down at the Brewery Site. Yet, typical of Mateer, there is a two-way process in play. As soon as you start reading, you realise that the psyche of these poems is local or regional only as a question of conscious choice, conscious perception. Sure, there are sunsets, bush, saltpans, surfies. But invoking a huge shift of dimension, the West is also that post–World War Two, socio-economic mega-project none of us anywhere has escaped from. To talk of 'the West' picks up this slightly dated, ex–Cold War connotation and shifts the ground which these poems reference. Global, IMF-dominated, ideological, it is a term for TV pundits and think-tank specialists. What we know about it is not so much what it means but what it cannot mean, for whatever else it may mean the West definitely cannot mean Third World or developing or sub-economic or black.

This game of small names played against over-arching names is a subtle current through Mateer's poems. Repeatedly in this selection we find poems which identify these 'non-western' features in the middle of the everyday world of, well, the West. By which I mean (in this instance) everyday life in the wealthy, resource-rich state of WA. Thus you could say that *The West* is neither just a worldly book in a global sense nor is it just a local book in an intimate sense. It is both. And on both planes, it is a book of fractures, of everyday moments threatening to split apart. A question about the nature of the West, its impact, its dispossessing force, its complexity and liberty and sophistication, troubles the heart of the poetic matter here as it has many of the poets who are Mateer's antecedents. I am thinking of the French Caribbean poet, Aimé Césaire or, closer to our own time, Derek Walcott or the Russian exile Joseph Brodsky. Mateer's work belongs in this larger world tradition of poetry written in and from displacement and exile, that state (or rather non-state) in which key perspectives not visible to the settled inhabitant become self-evident. Displacement for Mateer is not just national and external, but internal, in the mind. What can be claimed in the Westralian light of the present—and by whom—is a kind of stylistic tightrope which these compact, often epigrammatic, linguistically assertive poems balance along. Names, the need to name, the ability to name, are at the centre of this book.

Readers not previously familiar with John Mateer's poetry will in part find here a suburban world as widely spread as is any new city. In part, they will find the subjective, personal world of a poet searching for his historical and mythological context. Those of us who have been reading Mateer's work for the last fifteen years or so since the appearance of his first book will also recognise a consistent key element of his ongoing achievement—namely, his particular mix of blunt directness with, at the same time, a consciousness of how language is tricky and cannot easily or innocently be personalised. Reading him, we all become that reader he signals in one of the later poems in this book: this is the reader whose tongue hesitates to voice words blindly, even the words of the greatest, most stylish Imperial poets. Perhaps, he suggests, this hesitation is especially needed when faced with the words of the best, most memorable poets. Rippling throughout this selection, that sort of irony—the spreading rings of association around a deeply conscious attention to the act of writing and reading poetry—is one the great pleasures of looking at his poems. For his poetry is both confrontational and, at the same time, seductive and aesthetic. Yes, there is a personality, a grungy intelligence, a contemporaneity about his work; but, as a consequence, there is no room for a naivety or an indifference as to how the poem operates in the world. Yes, the poems are stylish, sharply written, voiced with great accuracy to their target, and at the same time they are inflected with a perennial sense of loss. It is a feeling maturely based in the search for deep attachments.

There is beauty, insight, acerb, epigrammatic ease, outburst and longing in this book. But, perhaps more than anything else, what underlies his poetry is a special sense of history, a particularly honest awareness of how the historical dimension of experience impinges on—'occurs'—in the present: literally in the present moment of awareness. Language is fast, ignorable, irrelevant within the dimension of pastness, and yet utterly necessary. The carefully chiselled tone, the careful placement of these poems in terms of larger poetic histories, are sufficient testimony to that. Experience is banal, intuitive, momentary and yet is pivoted on a recognition of huge, ramifying histories of settlement and exploitation: namely, on what Mateer calls in the collection's opening poem, 'violence'. Much Australian poetry flees from this sort of history. From Charles Harpur on, the emergent tradition of Australian poetry has powerfully reworked (and sometimes ironised) inherited poetic language, form and style but largely only as they derive from European and American antecedents. Other poets have re-positioned the long tradition of poetry after Romanticism which interlinks mind and environment: they have made this tradition our own, as a local, natural, Australian space. Mateer sidesteps both. While he treats style as a brilliant container for speech like any postmodernist might, he achieves a language of acute psychological sincerity and even pain. He seems to speak from nowhere as a sort of supra-national poet. Yet by the very same token he writes (as very few Australian poets can) with an on-the-pulse awareness of what it feels like to live out there, in some outlying Australian suburb, on the freeway, over there, truly in the West.

exile

THE PREMONITION

I attempt to peel the newspaper, but
it's soaked through with invisible
blood. I suppose there are birds to
knock their airy shells, though
I only hear crows creaking. Yesterday
seemed to be something else. I went
and saw art in an old asylum. The blue
and iron along West Coast Drive had
been scoured by thunder and mutely
glimmered. The people I saw stood up inside
their shadows, elongated thoughts of people
stretching to thoughts of bright day.
The premonition was that I'm asleep,
sleeping sensibly, believing it takes more
violence to wake us than daybreak.

FIRE IMAGINED

Past fire is present in thick grasstrees
chaotic with naturalism, prehistoric growth.

Someone said it's more intense in mind than
out there: towns divide the emptiness into distance,
graveyards beat the glare between shards of
flowerpot, weed and headstones that are bottled
heat.

It's like when last year my mother saw
an angel in the clouds.

Being realistic I told her in this heat it'd
melt before hitting the ground.

TWO YEARS AGO

When the locust plague
was supposed to infiltrate
the city we found a wing
on our driveway's black.
The interior of the land
had become a skin 'evidenced'
by the oily crystal of a dead
insect. It mightn't
have been that. We
drove down south, through
fields bristling with dark
life. They bopped on the window,
screeched against wipers. I
was stopped by two people
who said, "The creatures'll
eat anything if it's green."
There didn't seem to be
any green, just bleak
earth-shades breaking
into other light.

THE CANADIAN MEMORY

Along the St Lawrence River, through
dense thickets of hand-like twigs
in pockets of snow, we played games. The water
was a speeding sky that left the world behind
and gargled ice.
My great-uncle drove
trucks across the ice when the bridge
into Toronto was a log-jam of
cars tiptoeing on salt:

> *You keep the door open just in case…*

Some boy I never knew was torn away. Found
miles downstream by slow Mounties
in rubber boots.
　　　With smog the city warms
a white sky.

EPITHALAMIUM

Slowly injected with life, the roses on
my cousin's wedding dress fill, float.

The inverted city is a reflection. Her
buoyancy, epithalamium, lightness in the

sky—a tranquilised effect, or nervous
mirrors looking back?—is silence. Under

water we dance a sleepy tango to French
music that's soaking through the wall.

I saw the red moon. Tomorrow will come.
Her husband and I, no longer in goldmines,

will stand on the horizon, on the balls
of our feet,

     and blow cloud from Mauritius.

THE SIRENS' SONG
— for Noel Sheridan

Nipping the wine glass against his chest
with his stump of an arm, he shook my
hand. I'd met him before but he didn't
believe me. He nodded intensely, the
empty arm of his jacket slapping against
his side as he spoke to the man who'd
introduced me. "It was the sirens' song…"
My opinion changed its face. The other man
responded, his Irish accent both foreign
and clear: "Then the media got a hold
of the thing. They trotted out the wife,
tears, the drug-death and all that. Yes,
it was sad… The women in the bathroom,
some anamorphosis beyond belief, and it
was awful. Some of it had life: looking out
over Lavender Bay, the blue, and the flesh
of it all. Inevitable, you could see it…"
Moving the wine glass from his side, staring
across at me in the silence, tilting his head
back, eyes rolling, peeling back from
their prescription lenses, their jelly slowly
sopping deeply into the sockets, he said,
"They were calling him onto the rocks;
the sirens' song…"

THE CITY

Outside the Nightclub

With the intention of seeing
a gothic nightclub during the day
we had walked down an empty
street, speaking. Like a lucid
sketch, another skeletal street
hardened under the flesh of this
one. *Memory.* The disused neon
flashed under the flattened sky.
The sandstone architecture sailed
upward. She asked: "Where?" My
fingers clambered between hers.
At the very centre of her eyes
the pupils were black again.

The Word

Meat-flower: the word I use for the sex of your
mouth. Terminal moraine dumped from my
tongue. Cairns, images from my grandmother's
dream, a house of clocks ticking an irregular
ocean, chaotic waves mountainous,
black:

　　　On heaped sand the girl in the silver dress
fluttered. In a backyard a small dog leashed
to brickwork barks. I stand. Parallel to my
shoulders, my one hand holds your heavy
flowers and I feel stars picking specks
from my eyes.

　　　Between midnight and midday
and midnight, I could have quoted, but
those stones, subtle and better left unsaid,
are flowers of their own. In the other room
we smile at your gran as she fills glasses of
water, polishes mirrors and knows to
hide.

Strolling in the Supreme Court Gardens

Here, strolling, if that's what legs
do at three o'clock in the morning,
I can remember—

under arching trees
two lovers, close into themselves,
struggle further.

The brackish river blackens,
shoves itself into a sound.

I can imagine swans, dark swans alive
with flame across live
water: stars.

Stop.
      The cranial planetarium is
drunkeness. Squeezed between gates,

we enter the Supreme Court Gardens.

Velvet-mouthed spotlights exhale, yawn,
scratch teeth on scrawny branches,
iodine-stench, shadow.

Around green sight our eyes slide
to sculpt flowers, erectile tulips
all bony and incandescent.

You thumb the Roman numerals
and murmur, your voice resembling
silence:

"The sundial's at midnight."

Her face… her face, atomic, is
translucent, another woman's.

Moonless

Through thinning darkness we emerged
under the fairy-lights of a backyard, out

into the road where houses are shapes
and the sky is negative, white.

Then hours. I realise your car is
black, not a star-like red. With two voices

we ask: "Where should we go?" The closer
I get the more I must push

my feet towards the ground: light-headed,
cold. "To The Moon," I answer. (*Who are you?*)

Artaud said: *I am on the moon*
as others are on their balconies.

I wonder if he had ever loved...
It's not like an answer. I spin around:

"There's no moon tonight."

It's so clear.

The Eye

His eternally disembodied eye
over the lighted desert,
like an icon glaring down
from the corner against
the ceiling, down on all
the hands in the room. His
is the eye that counters
astrophysics with presence;
and the blackhole won't
relent, is as holy as the
shudders—FEAR—peeling of
skin as I fuck her
from behind and her breasts shrug
and on our eyes sight fades.
Only when I have dreamed of
suicide has an eye like that
turned on its side and melted
down her face.

At a Yellow Bench

I could retract. She gnaws an apple, frowning.
The city is half blocked from our view by
giant slabs of fake marble: the State Library.

She tells me two friends have suicided. Not
friends: *acquaintances…* She is slowly
chewing. We wear leather shoes. The

Abstraction—death is abstract, isn't it?—is
my response: "We seem to contain it."
She says, "Oh," as though it could cease there.

But death, mute death, heavy in my scrotum
like a jewel, can be ignored. I lift my arm
behind her, imperceptible. The parody

of my saying—. She says, "It seems so…"
Then irritatedly shudders. Not even a sigh. "It
looks like Perth ten years ago."

"Without the skyscrapers you mean?" I ask.
We wait. She glides away.
We seem as blank as the city.

EXILE

She spoke about the beautiful country,
where you wouldn't think those things
would happen, where Kurds live in
black tents on plateaux I have imagined.

She told us about her father's friend
who was tortured, having hot oil
splattered in his armpits, molten light
rippling over scar-tissue, burning a mouth.

And I thought of comparable tortures,
those I'd read of and my friends in
other countries that I can't imagine.
And I said nothing. I thought:_____.

ON HISTORY

By hearing his own words
and staring into the mirror
he learns the person
they think he is. He had
always wanted to say, *History
is given,* but as he thought
on what that might mean he
felt silence would be safer
and knew the face in the
mirror was too clear.

(MIRROR)

That person they see
I sometimes imagine

behind two eyes,

winking, a face
silvery in the mirror.

among the australians

CONVERSATION

I spoke to the Australian poet,
asking him if the poems came
from the same place in space

and time. "No," he said, "each
poem is from a different space.
So if you imagine this room

as a brain, one poem would be
there, another there." He seemed
to see what he was thinking…

I saw only a cloud, a black cloud-
stone up against the ceiling,
an exhaling Venus of Willendorf.

THE DRUG SCENE

At a Party

When the surveyor held her arms,
dragged her into the lounge and
closed the door, she thought they were
going to attempt rape. But what they
wanted to ask was the time and
if she was going to wear that white
dress, the one with gold spirals
that look as if embroidered of her
hair.

In an Alley

They watched her in the alley
when she lay down, crucified,
on a painted white arrow. And walked
around the block so that she could

sober up: "At the moment I'm hallucinating
and I need someone to be nice
to me..." As they walked from there she
yelled, called a silhouetted man

by his name. Standing at the half-
opened car door, his face unlit,
raw, he stared. She shouted: "Got any
speed?" "Shshsh." Then haggled. They

watched, heard cloud steaming behind a wall.
Also looked when she showed him,
by the ailing light of his glove-box, where
they had stabbed her trying to find a vein.

NOUMENA

It feels like my mind
is morphing my body again. That
I will become all
Mind. So

through my window
I watch the square
of sky and see how clouds are patiently
defused by wind. I say,
in distraction:

    Ek wil soos 'n wolk wees.

~

Wo bist Du, mein Traum?
Wo bist Du…

While under my feet
        there were those zones of pain
where blisters
        haven't yet appeared.

~

Bent-necked, with teeth clenching
the strap to squeeze
her hard arm, bring a vein
to fruition for
one slow injection,
she has the face,
the one face she always has
when concentration
evenly dispersing, bloating
the worn skin, is like that
slow-motion video of an
atomic explosion.

~

We were fucking
in my dream. She

was pale, Japanese, smiling
through eyelids tilted

by indivisible sighs.
She was my colourless mind.

Like taken breath,
she sank over me.

We were both so whole
we couldn't move.

WAITING FOR THE BARBARIANS

When playing soccer with the child, I was
conscious of the hills of houses, suburbs spreading
like the fat of age around emotion's
gut. Another day digested as unnoticed dusk
slid past the vacant lots and limestone blocks, trundling
sand to slip into the low, unmarked ocean soundless
with anti-freeze, anti-rust. This broad emptiness
I felt as a Greek in Alexandria, hearing
the zone's houses and my parents' home boxing-in
unfleshed bodies, seeing
what I couldn't see—

a house like a ship full of white walls.

"...HERMES IS TO BLAME"

— for Brian McKay and my late father

THE VISIT

Through the usually open doorway
of his house I see him. "G'day, Young John!"
I greet him, too. A smile.
Death is always over the threshold,
'a dark horse', as I was called yesterday. While
we wait for boiling water, tinkling crockery, busying silence,
I page through a book of aerial photos. Settlements
of different societies. He shows me a photocopy
of an acquaintance's obituary:
classicist, foreign-correspondent, poet:
"We'd shared a house with a now famous
guitarist friend, and they'd all demonstrated against
the dictatorship in Greece. Later he lived on the top floor, over
a fruiterer's shop. He never
had money, all his books were on stolen Coke crates,
and he slept in a sleeping-bag, fed
on given fruit." Silently I
read the excerpt from one of his poems.
"It seems to me," I'm saying, "that there's nothing to
resolve. My generation"—I'd just finished reading *The Philosophy
of Money*—"is either blasé or cynical." He tells me, another friend,
a mild-tempered philosopher, is totally ignored, reminiscent
of an exile during the Roman Empire, in Africa! Then
another's anecdote:

"No one wanted to buy the series of stainless-steel pyramids.
In passing, they were pure reflection, a collapsing
of visibilities. So he had a bulldozer excavate trenches,
and buried them. Then the potential buyer came, wanted to see them.

"You can buy them, he'd said. *They're there…*
According to tests, they'll last twenty-three thousand years."

When I was about to leave, he spoke about his son:
"He died of a lesion on the brainstem. The gradual paralysis
began in his feet and worked its way up until he
was like a frozen corpse."

My friend is looking older, his age…

I vow to write as nobly as that dead man.

The Message

My father had been in another shape, a traumatic
avatar, when his finger was nicked on the uncurling
sardine-can lid. *To halt the bleeding hold
the limb higher than the heart.* Lay
on the couch, near hysterical,
his hand over his face. For two days the wound
pinched with pain.
        Using binoculars, he
looks out over the hills of houses, viewing,
there above the whirlybird of the roof
in front, the city's two tallest buildings.

In the doctor's waiting-room I read of an
advisory committee—linguists, scientists, artists—who've
decided monoliths incised with languages, equations,
cartoons, would be best to
warn people in ten- or maybe a hundred-thousand years
that nuclear waste is buried
near.
    "Trying to find compatible marrow
is like playing the lottery…" The doctor,
depressing a large syringe, smears five slides with
darkness.

    *I want to be a traditional Tiwi
singing of the Japanese bombardment of Darwin*

    *In song I want to be embraced
by the legs and arms of a girlfriend*

At home, in a long passage, I sit cross-legged,
copying something onto a large sheet of white—

HERMES IS TO BLAME.

THE TOWER

Brick by brick the convent's Romanesque bell-tower
was unbuilt, transported, then rebuilt.
Saved from an erasing that could invoke
the Rainbow Serpent's curse on the property
of Australia's richest woman, the Thirties
edifice posing on the Northbridge corner around which
ragers out for a huge night swirl, that awkward nose
of baked-sand-without-a-bell in front of Vultures
café in the yellow Taxation Precinct—built
by the same richest woman—lacks an earthed face.
Architecturally an immigrant bastard, an orphan,
he provokes a story: "Remember? Think it was Bropho.
He warned them the demolition
would disturb the Wagyl… You know, I remember
a rainy night when I was going to see an
exhibition of paintings from Utopia and I could have
seen that guy, The Husband. I think he was then the
second or third richest man in Australia. I couldn't go, though.
Too far to catch the bus. It was
just after that he died. Of a heart-attack, they
say. I say: THE SNAKE. People say, Yeah-yeah: Didn't
he have a family history of heart-complaints?
I say: Yeah. In a city where whole buildings
walk like chess-pieces…"

THE SURFER

Into the telephone my surprised
housemate was saying he'd
seen fist-fucking, that
the limb looked senseless,
like a fleshy wing. This was
the same guy who—in the
middle of an operation—had
stopped breathing, whose
heart had stopped, was officially
dead, the surfer who dreamed
of the ideal swell and taped
up countless posters of
blue and perfectly riderless waves.

THE NORM

But when I saw her,
'my first fuck',
in the supermarket, both
of us doing our weekly chore,
the place polished by fluoro-green
was not so much a
maze as a gallery
of itemised lust. *Here's*
a black pen, draw barcodes on
my forehead. Quickly. She's
passing… I'd had visions:
maternal heritage strobed
from her flesh that night,
her loosened bra revealed indifferent,
if glowing, lunar skin. My heart
was singing like dawn birds in
established suburbs.
She took my virginity into
her with a tough kitchen-hand's grip,
gnawed me with muscle.
I: her one-nighter after a band and
too much beer. She: my longing
randomised. The one guarantee
here in this supermarket
in this exchangeable city is
the face's inevitable
sighting me, then turning,
the daze normal.

(BRIEF DIGRESSION ON POIESIS)

Only by devastation are
we seen in
the bushland. Our
daemons—thought as
water, sand furrowing
open to granular
sighs—don't slow to
reflect that this
Hell of our Making, even
if we meditate
on 'a random branch',
feels like
evaporation by one
atomic sun.

MOMENT

By a trick of afternoon light, a
mirror and a window, I saw

my yellow mouth hover over
one eye.

~

I opened the mouth:

air
was displaced.

~

The certainty
of that golden monster biting
oxygen was a blinding
another would ignore—

THE SUNLIT ROOM

Her Ethiopian Crucifix

On the raised bed we offered
ourselves: nerves gathered in fingers, scrolls
of skin were handholds, genitals
swelling in hushed expression, tongues
lush with tastebuds, the dense
scent. When I'd stood watching
her on the bed, her lying with back
propped by her elbows, I had wished
for a photographic memory. I had told her I'm always
embarrassed by poems that aren't specific enough:
How could I describe her to my own mind,
let alone to the past world? Like that
I loved her, her Thirties hairstyle, the freckles
on her face and in the crescent of
her chest where Thai sunlight scorched
the usually pale flesh, those eyes—their green
similar to mine—that scan newsprint, the Albany
sunrise and my face… I studied the moles on
her unfreckled places. Like stars enlarged
by a sensual astronomer's eye. Most vivid, though,
I don't know why, was that Ethiopian crucifix
hanging from its leather thread on
the back of her neck.

My Name

Too far away to climb, the mountain is
shimmering day. At the base of my
spine, vertebrae like eroded teeth. My
face is distant, chest a murmur. *I...*

I climbed up the dome behind the house yesterday,
heard one road-train dragged out into space.
My silent voice: *The Continuous had
their throats slashed...* My girlfriend,

though I'm not sure she would use that word,
is stressed-out, working. Bright country
air becomes the panoramic distance's
chill. The white cat, mouthing her

morning voice, meows my name, my one name...

THE LONG MAN OF WILMINGTON
— for Brian Blanchflower

In Albany's night sky I saw it: the depth
of black stars, pores in a transparent face.

We could have been on a green, almost
invisible, knoll. The Long Man of Wilmington,
chalk tracks flickering gracefully

on the facing scarp, walking as though
rising, striding, weakly flashing attention-

inattention, knocking through constellations.
He had said: "That's exactly what I felt,
that you were him, you were the hill." Whale-rocks

sank under the exhaling tide of gusty shrubs,
a ghost dolphin was released on dark sparkling
that's neither chewy blood nor Memory's black.

For me there remains a human-sized space.

the nature

TASMANIAN OBSERVATIONS

Devils Gullet

In staring down, our sight becomes falling rock,

those precipice walls the edge of a glacial tongue that
calves—with rupturing like pistol shots in a courtyard—
icebergs huge as thirty-storey buildings.

The leaden shockwaves, of ice on ocean water,
of boulders on valley rock, can't be heard,

except as distant, raspy gusts.

On the Plateau

Buttongrass moorland, edged by snow gums,
is still as an unbreathing mouth. Here the air's thinner than membrane.

My heart accelerates at the sight: *One ice-tipped mountain.*

An imported zero is exactly this: *The exhilaration of the plateau,*
afferent, like memories from a beloved photo.

Visitors Centre

The thylacine, in hologram,
returns from annihilation
as a watery green wraith,
a dim luminous incarnation
observed between two umwelts
in a blue forest of nerves.

SPLITTER FALLS, LORNE

This footpath flowing along the ledge
raises me against the cliff face
over a gorge whose
rapids aren't seen behind the trees.
Morning clear with the qualia
of foliage, the unreflecting white waters
that chug like blood past shut ears.
Across from here, across the deep gash
abraded by the invisible river,
a thin tributary is gushing,
splattering flat black rocks
to coalesce with the wrong gravity.
From oceanic mouths rivers should stream
back to thunderheads; mountains should
again be granular, and cold planets gas.
We should see that and be cautious, silence.
On this gorge's other side
cumulus gums sough. Spotting them,
I'm mossy, inhaling consciously.
Those white birds gliding there, sulphur-crested
cockatoos, are the pit of my stomach in lift-off.
Then they perch. They're airborne
again, then perch. Like pebbles trying to
bed down in the river, like giant cycads
tensioning a spider's thread. Under
decaying leaves, bark, wood
and aspirating soil we are already extinct.
No need to widen eyes or wait.
Every step's a rock pool, then a waterfall.
This well-worn path pulls my feet along.

TOWARDS WILPENA POUND

When salt and bluebush country
gives way to the small yellow constellations of
wattle, the mind enters existence. Then

native pines stand—where rabbits had cleared the undergrowth
and where they themselves were wiped out by an island virus—
echoing plantations. Further, in the sung wind,

subtle bodies are a glimmer, fluid as the invisible river
over broken rock geometry, as extinction.
The sentence, then, is an unrealisable mountain.

ON A COASTAL WALK

Trudging across an inlet with the winter tide rushing in
my boots slurping the sand
the water detonating then foaming and fanning over the hump of beach
over my boots the cold surface bubbling forever and an instant
like trillions of equidistant molecules between which *this*
was annihilated—

MULLALOO

Every hot day while I was up there
the shimmering beach would have me floating on haze
or bodysurfing the uterine waves' edge

And every day I'd be passing
bushes pale with dust, cars rusting into sand,
passing on feet bejewelled with granules that
are a Melbournian skin whiter than their previous stone

And what I noticed was what a friend
had previously photographed in a meticulous panorama before
these infinite suburbs were even
twinkling in one developing eye, before I even knew which country
would be mine, I saw

not the caprock, limestone teeth raised where
vanished vegetation tapped and sucked holding a dune

not pinnacles left like dolmen in *Europa*, like
hard glare in a tourist's glance, No,

I saw
those stone outbreaks as the rough scales
of the thorny-devil lizard on whose back we're lifted.

AT GNANGARA

Trees ringbarked. Underbrush set alight.
Then the charcoal bones chained, pulled to the ground,
ploughed in: the sand turning belly up.

The grey dirt of erasure is planted with pine saplings.
Their acidic needles bed down thickly.
Dark regimented trunks and a stifling silence,

maybe one raven cawing. The smothered seeds
wait. (To awaken them scarify or pop in hot water,
though often that doesn't work.) Then bushfire

reduced the plantation to ash. After thirty years,
like a nation after decades of martial law,
bodies unclenching, eyes opening, native seeds are sprouting.

BROADCASTING

The fertilised banksia blooms harden into cones, dark ovals
ribbed with nodules, indestructible, their procreant vaults

emerging like small clenched eyes.

When the living fire comes, the flames advancing in a scraggly line,
like Emergency Services people searching for a lost child,

then, coming into its own, the cone can undo its silence

and open into one black yoni whose whole body is
dry parted lips naturally spitting out seeds.

CASUARINA, THE WORD

The word is a gaol, a plot of land, a tree
and a cassowary. When we heard,
we didn't name that sound
as a cry, a call or a song.
Maybe a cow, a fox, a devil
or a cassowary? Not an emu in the guise
of a sizzling tree, nor Macassan
eyes mistaking the she-oak's feathered
branches for the wings of a cassowary.

ODE

Kangaroo-paw,
scarlet dipstick measuring
the depth of blood in which we live,
Bloom like one of those small
marsupial limbs appearing
redundant, shrunken
like the head of an enemy,
and yet like a rabbit's foot, an amulet—
These resemblances in a skull's museum are
not recognition, are the oxygenated
blood of living memories.

AFTERMATH

        Walk into my mouth,
into the head that isn't mine.
        Sit cross-legged on the crinkly, sooty ground,
on the wisps of singed hair
in the aftermath. Undamagingly

ironic isn't this? that arsonists
with their seed-flames hidden
often help fight the inferno,
        as if enacting an atavistic memory of
firestick farming.

Another irony pushed out the front of my mind or mouth
        —the few leaves that weren't vanquished,
visible as 'crisps' in this windlessness,
are almost the colour of their deciduous relatives...

Slender, leafless antennae of dissident green
        sprout. Low grasstree fronds
fluorescent in dim space. Like hackles
        rising close to the body, from she-oaks'
        bark static electricity...

        I approach a tree,
trying to tell its type from reptilian
evenly scaled charcoal skin:
apartheid? Near my hand on the bark, an ant.
In its jaw-hands a huge load of food.

THE SCAR-TREE OF WANNEROO

Near Lake Joondalup's untouchable burning whiteness,
midst the outer suburban industrial parks and contemporary pioneer homes,
on the dry grassy verge of Frederick Road, Wanneroo,
the old but still living tree that wasn't torn down in the early days
to be duckboards for the road heading north
through the scrubby sandplains shimmering in mind,
that wasn't bulldozed yesterday for another optimistic space,
bears scars where bark was prised off
for a coolamon or shield or piece of shelter.
This oldman-tree might elsewhere have been a hallowed thing,
garlanded, smoked-in with incense, imminent,
a series of photos of blue, cloudless sky. But here
this jarrah, fragmenting heart isn't one of many milestones
measuring out an historic silence, an empty hurt.
In mind, this almost forgotten memory, this in-grown wounding,
is not the last in a country of countless scar-trees.

DUSK

The tree had exploded, shattered
showering this path in brittle
fragments, bonewhite.

I wasn't sure where the path went.

There was the non-existent tree
bloodshot in the World's Eye;
a space you couldn't cross.

I went around to where I am to sleep
where kangaroos will be seen like
one clapping hand and above the clouds
an aeroplane drags out a thundery din.

Near, in a lone she-oak: *prana.*

Around us, the virgin wandoo
like cold white-skinned apparitions gathering
for Law are receding
deeper, closer than sight.

THE MANY-FACED MOUNTAIN

The Stirling Ranges

As though the oceanic waters,
like sleep, are palpable in absence
and dream, geologically
inferred, in tidal withdrawal
from the plain, through rivers' mouths
spoke the word MOUNTAINS,
abandoning silt in heaps,
quaking earth up
in a harmonic range
extending from this rounded mound
to the brain-wavey haze
in the distant blue-washed crags
and worn-tooth ridges;
these hills growing as I
drive the park's boundary road,
expanding as sound must
or collapsing like gas
in a star's birth. On one side,
the fence, kangaroo-brown sheep, dust-industry,
on the other, jolts squiggled in rock,
the complications plants live by,
and my unchained, happy, breathable mind:

I drive into the mouth, into bright silence.

The Walk Up

On their haunches these crags and bluffs and peaks
are solid not fluid as us in our pervious
skin. They crouch. At the foot of the highest

as I'm leaving the carpark to begin the walk up I
see what my father would have seen when he was here—
memories of another mountain
projected like a slide-show onto the wall of this one.
I had already read the 'alleged' story for this place.

And as I'm walking, climbing, my steps confident and
legs fulfilled, my psyche is transparent cloud.

This path crosses dry streams.

Any mountain is a view into the invisible.

To think that they call this a 'knoll'!

Up here I'm lying across an outcrop
looking down the cliff face. The updraft cutting.

Here I lie in mourning. Here two wedge-tailed eagles
gliding in the swinging gusts
gently bump. Fallibility.
The tourists exchange smiles.
I'm looking south, coastwards.

Near this range, on the farmland plain,
saltlakes flat and white as huge blisters on
the splayed toes of the woman whose ground we're under.
This mountain her heel. Stretching out
from here holes jabbed
by her hungry digging-stick.

Out on a Saltlake

Walking out onto the saltlake
from the screen of tattered paperbarks
and the intermittent groundcover
of samphire strands. Under my boots

the surface is like new cement
and each sloppy step resists its
record. Behind me slime filling
the heels of my footprints.

Like being on a winter beach after
the tide's gone out. On this overcast day
sun and mountain breathe briny air.
An emu and a man have left their tracks.

Argument

Could still have been thinking
our language, my being, is like
a legless lizard, word appendages
defunct in this new terrain,
when on this narrow path out
to the promontory a metre-long
goanna stopped me.

With a twisted branch I poked it.
Wouldn't move.
Threw a chunk of wood.
It raised its head.
Blinked.
Still wouldn't move.
Threw more wood.

Its snake-face opened jaws to silence.

I am being told something.

I tried to force it along, stamping
but it wouldn't leave the track.
It ran further up the track.

Its pink-mouthed obstacle was an argument.

The Haunted

Like the hunted I am paralysed,
the spirit-become-meat in a Nepali poem,
calcium in a laboratory. On this secluded
beach, on the promontory's Southern Ocean side
sinking water explodes against
fissured basalt slabs, grey undulations spray white.

A whale's vertebra abandoned.

(Coda)

Stooped I approach you.

You: *The Many-Eyed-Mountain.*
You: *All-Eyes.*

You sense me. I stop.

Standing here like a tree stump.
Standing here with my arms shrunken and lame.

As I am stooped the misty corpse may not see me.
I am stooped and my eyes unblink.

I am invisible.

> *To the hunting, I am a mountain.*
> *To you, I may not exist.*

Stepping as carefully as I'm breathing

I approach, and you approach me,
PLACE-OF-DEATH. I am invisible.

You sense me. I stop.

LAST NIGHT

Last night, in lucid dreaming, I
was a black cockatoo, one
of those heard sharp as a moon sliver
but couldn't be seen under the high
Southern Cross. I was naked,
shaggy with feathers, and lifting
one foot, then another, flexing, looking
around the branches' fretwork
under the roof of leaves. I
was uneasily considering if I had the right perch.

mokare's ear

THE QUESTION

To Mudrooroo

I saw you at Wisdom Books buying Buddhist texts
I saw you at the Writers Festival mocking all the palefaces

Is your Kurdaitcha Man a sing-song, a Jackie or a Johnnie?

I heard you in your novel—there were blackfellas on Cottesloe Beach
staring at white girls vulnerable in malicious light

I heard you laughing with two black ladies as they told stories
of their youth and games and stealing oranges and the mission school

Will you ever recognise yourself in my face and voice?

Let me tell you—

My friend's brother-in-law used to call your people
'boongs', used to summon with that word an evil

And you know what? He was camping near a sacred site
up north *And you know what?* He saw strange lights hovering there

and couldn't shed his WHITENESS

Could our silence be as real and deep as that?

To Jack Davis

Sweltering in the tent at the Writers Festival,
the dramatist and elder,
his eyes milky under the brim of his akubra,
answers the question with another:

You have your own culture.
Go back to the Greeks.

IN REAL TIME

Payback is how
we are ghosts, I thought
on the freeway void
and infertile as the European idea
of desert. (I was speeding
towards the city
of sky-scraping shards.)

~

For a split-second
behind closed eyes:

open country.

~

At the dark Brewery Site
I close my eyes,

knowing that now, in a dare,
some young men
are probably adrenalised, dreaming,
scaling the 120 metre high TV transmitter
to steal the warning-light's
　　　red,
threaten low flying planes.

THE BREWERY SITE

Up here in the Botanical Garden
I am descending an informal path
to the wire fence
that throws my ghost over—

~

At the foot of this hill,
snaking through the sprawled body of this city,

the Swan River is a shimmering,
expanding blindness.

~

Now I'm down there beside the expansive glare,
looking at a trough of green water.

Perth's first public spring, the sign tells me.

Silence cordons off the day: EFFACEMENT.

~

The sacred can't be apparent.

~

Behind me, between the demolished white man's school
and the whispering grove of London plane trees,
there isn't space,
only time, unspeaking.

~

In my peripheral vision I am walking towards the Old Swan Brewery,
I am crossing the diaphanous, sizzling traffic of Mounts Bay Road
and am witnessing my dissolute self
in a Bibbulmun sacred place.

~

Years ago, on TV,
I saw landrights protesters in a scuffle with police here.

I've been told passing drivers
would toot in solidarity with the Nyoongars.

I can easily envisage the elders teaching their children here,
telling them how the Wagyls

invoked the city's lakes and rivers,
then dove into the fount,

~

vanished.

~

"Look out there, across the waters,
over what's seen through startling photons.

Look beyond that river and sky,"
I tell myself, "identify your corpse."

~

But on this shore the Brewery
is only brick and glass,
walled-in shadow,
apartments awaiting their ghosts.

~

I close my eyes, let my voice walk away.

I sit down on the paving at the water's edge,

asking myself,

~

Am I weeping, an anachronism?

~

(Around someone on the riverbank
vanquished, translucent paperbarks gather like the grieving.)

THE WORD

His joke: the whip of roobar
against dark flesh: BOONG.

The national dictionary explains
its origins as *Bahasa*:

BUNG: friend, comrade, or mate.

TALKING WITH YAGAN'S HEAD

After Reading

Drawn down the sulphur-yellow sand embankment,
down from the sticky bitumen of the parking area out the front
of the new tent-shaped shopping centre,
across the road and down into the white limestone glare,

I was in a secluded ditch, freed from being myself, that human.
I didn't feel like the artist who looked at woodchips,
felt himself fragmenting. I watched the trees.
Like derelict people, cracked by living, part-charred
by bushfire breath. I kept describing this
to myself: *the balga: 'grass fountains'.*
             the mooja: 'like elephant trunks'. I
wanted
to dig down for the parasitic encirclements around other roots.
They taste like candy. I wanted to crack open
a balga, look for bardi in case I'm ever
lost—

       Then I was thinking, talking: *See that giant banksia there,*
that huge beauty that looks like a dinosaur's friend?
Bull banksia, mangite—
And I was walking around seeing benevolent flames atop
balga spikes, on the banksia cones.

I knelt down and found a seedling—"Marri"—and a softening
banksia finger patterned like plaid. Between my four thumbs it crumbled.
A brown fibre. Looks and smells like snuff.
"Looks and smells like snuff," I told myself, asking
who I told.

    I told myself: "In this place you're talking with Yagan's Head."

The City's Heart

The brown speckled jellyfish, silk-stocking smooth,
pulsed at the water's edge. The still beating heart
of an invisible scavenger. I look back
up the riverbank hoping no one'll take my bag.

As I approach the river
trees, hooking their branches low,
have roots grasping the earth, squeezing
the clay like food in infants' fists,
spreading the soil over every surface,
smearing black on faces.

Beyond me is the glittering—shadowing, ghosting—of our shapeless
river.
      Humid; now the breeze. Leaves inhale, meditate.
      My mind, panoramic, now—(then) seeing

night's VOID river, sees in the lava-slow water,
deserts red with marnta blood, tongues forking with pejorative names
reclaimed for meaning.
The CD sound of Pintipi voices through my shell. Then—'I'

      want to say, *Boong, white man as boong: Kaffir.*
But the city on the other side of the hill won't look at me.

To Sing Outside

Karark!

Black cockatoos
you are the same sight I have always seen
from storm clouds
like shadows carillonned out, a
fly-past
in warning.

Karak!

I have seen youse
streaking into the wind
shrieking all
together, like a sheet metal
shack tearing at
the gale's throat.

Kar-rak!

Like a feathered god
whose face is not expression
whose voice is not
this—DISTANT—counting between
electrical crack and
thunderclap.

Koorak!

THAT HOAX

Remember the heiress, princess of the Squattocracy,
who posed as a blackfella landscape painter,
and who when revealed claimed she was possessed
by the spirit of HE WHO NEVER EXISTED—

IN THE PRESENCE

Fifteen Songs

    Yagan,

Even if I stab a bloody gumtree you will not speak.

       ~

    Yagan,

The tree doesn't say, *Once I married the earth to the sky*.
And its branches don't say, *Once we sang with the wind*.

    The ghosts of the spoken are this huge tree
    on which every leaf is a silenced language.

The leaves don't mutter in passing, falling,
We are not regret. We are nutrients, slowly releasing…

    Nor does the bark respond;
the strips are scarified, flayed, a shredded document.

      ~

Yagan,

Won't your syrupy blood, instead of sap, ooze out
globules on the scabby trunk, sensitive as small tumours,
malleable and dark as molten glass.

And later won't that congealed blood, that brittle gum,
be tapped from the tree,
locals smearing that new sticky flow onto their weeping wounds.

~

Yagan,

Avatar, you are that moment of déjà vu
when in the early days of settlement your people
embraced, not the invaders,
but the ancestors returning in their ghostly skin.

~

Yagan,

Even you were 'reincarnated'—*a whiteman!*—once.

~

Yagan,

Your severed head shipped to the Old World,
exhibited as a trophy at which the subjects could gawp.

Your demonised head unknowingly they buried,
mistaking the skull for a time-capsule, a mirror sans images.

Your buried head brought out into Westralian glare
provoked an alien to hymn you in 1999.

~

Yagan,

In our nascent republic this poet would learn that your head,
no longer in a museum, was buried in an unmarked grave
with the stillborn. This poet witnessed your reclaimer on TV

heckling the Prime Minister who then called the elder in for a conference
behind the smoky glass of the limousine
where the powers-that-be whispered intimations of thunder.

~

Yagan,

He who is scribing these words
abandoned your country, the bushland that awoke his senses.

He who is singing this sentence
fled while archeologists were probing the riverbank
for your discarded body.

He shot through when the day was alive with a calm blindness,

vanished when the airport was the site
where a few of your mob, before they flew off to retrieve your shrinking
head,
had disputed genealogies and rights and verged on a punch-up.

~

Yagan,

One elder, while supporting—YOUR SKULL—his corner of the crate,
declared that in the island kingdom
a Wagyl had journeyed with.

He blamed the princess' carcrash death on her empire's karma.

Police divers were trawling the Swan River for your 60 kilo head.

(Here I must wonder if in our mind's eye
that private ceremonial island strewn with strangers' wreaths
was actually yours.)

~

Yagan,

When with the whispering of a fine-tooth hacksaw
your bronze statue was again beheaded
the moon was ocular, flushed,
and the black sound-waves encircling your island
were silences, hissing, hellish.

~

Yagan,

Without you the city is a ruin of broken glass,
like bottlenecks cemented along a decaying wall.

Without you the river at night is an opencast mine
where dreams are pornographic and Reconciliation is fire.

Without you the bankrupt are heroes and news-crews historians
because even your elders are suffering aphasia.

Without you this voice fears too few will notice
that poems, memorials and new constitutions are our sorrybooks unsigned.

~

Yagan,

A poet once, the apostate, she who'd abandoned the convent,
told her lover that years before,
when kneeling on the bone-chilling stone floor of a crypt in France,
praying to the Virgin while in sight of the saint's relic,
she awoke to a clarifying absence
and almost asked herself—

What am I doing here on my knees before a brown severed head?

Thus: the power of your absence.

~

Yagan,

Like the sooty tuning-fork prongs of trees after a bushfire,

you, to whom these words are sung, are a silence.

Addressed through this muted song,

you are more intimate than prayer, closer than my own flesh.

~

Yagan,

There was the dream in which your skull
and your skeleton were laid in state

and there were indistinguishable mourners
queuing to glimpse you before the next thieves' arrival.

~

Yagan,

Though the past is as anxious as native vegetation in the suburbs
and as intoxicating as a carton of petrol held under a child's nose,
you, your mythical head synonymous with space,
your abandoned body identical to time,
are the blackhole of words for which the Prime Minister
may apologise with these poems.

Envoi

(In the dusk, in Kings Park, I'm running)

The hero's remains will be returned tomorrow.

(seeing ahead of me, through the silent bushland of skin)

(that severed head glowing,

lighting this path)

PINJARRA

Down at the site of the battle which was more like a slaughter
some Nyoongar blokes showed him the crossing
where, there low over the blackened water,
they'd seen that fireball hovering white as a blind eye,
and he'd asked them if they'd tried to call out to those spirits
and they'd laughed:

    "No way, mate, we was off like a shot!"

invisible cities

THE NULLARBOR

Dusty eagles, leviathans of the scalding air, rise
from roadside corpses, wings truck windscreen-wide,
and flap across the eye of the roadtrain. The driver,
perched high in his cabin, sweating a waterfall,
sees the fable of the trucker crashing into a whole mob of camels,
sees the same Japanese cyclists passing him either
way across the Treeless Plain. He stops at a roadhouse,
swaps stories with the woman there. She saw two dark red
men driving a small ute down the middle of the highway
with a boxing roo squeezed between them.

ADELAIDE

The city's grid is a mirrored maze
surrounded by parkland only wide enough
to deter Russian cannonballs. Proudly
free of convicts, punctuated by statues
of a grimacing warhorse and four metre archangel,
office blocks crowd around Victoria Square.
There the Empress of Pink Maps faces away
from the tram to the palindromic beach.
And there, fleetingly sighted by sly tourists' eyes,
blackfellas down from the Red Centre
shout in language that ricochets off the mirrored walls.

THE BLACK ARMBAND OF MEMORY

One of the Earthrings at Sunbury

Like a large grassed-over plate, the earthring is almost invisible,
an upturned lip of dirt, an O, like an invocation in a pantheist's poem,
yet also banal, this site of men's initiation
fenced-in by the bright clear-cut architecture of outer suburban dreams.

    A memorial, a sanctuary, archaic post-object art?

I sit cross-legged just outside the ring whispering a dharani.

Notice that? Faint, the whirring traffic on the freeway, the slight tilt
of the ring towards the city's sparkling skyline, the bay's silence
and the boring khaki plains that are rising up
to me here, to this ring and to the vanished feet that would have been
—more than a Noh play's concluding (*stamp!*)—
an African pulsation, an Ancestral dance…

    What is this history? a dematerialising?

even as I, an alien, a haunting, bow down to the empty ground.

Visiting the Site of a Shell Midden

We are not more than they, wrote the Romantic on blackfella absence.
On our annihilation, too.

What kind of landmark is a vanished midden?

Tens of thousands of shellfish corpses piled as remembered conversations, banquets,
a minimal architecture, an opera house of ears or echoes.

What of this place, this life? that's not

the earlier natural order — COMMUNE — dreamt
by the early morning walkers, dingoes and silver gulls at misty Point Ormond
where the Elwood Canal, once a vocal wetland, is

quietly draining into The Bay,
where the midden was ancient garbage, is now evidence.

We are not more than they. And we believe that
they are here, will be here —

But who are they?

Who are we?

Who are you?

NOCTURNE

That evening no Vietnamese voices enlivened the Footscray streetscape,
only shopfront signs gesticulating: *This! This!*
So we, after a dinner of noodle soup and spring rolls, were disbelieving.

From restaurant windows our reflected faces watched us.

"Good morning Vietnam!" shouted someone like an actor,
a man in a bomber jacket and battered akubra, a veteran,
striding up the other side of the street towards us.

He hadn't. To the deserted street, again: "Go back to Vietnam!
Go back to Vietnam!" he yelled at two men
who ignored him, crossing the street.

Then he was following the young woman in jeans and high-heels.
"Why don't you go back?" she shouted over her exposed shoulder
"Why don't you go back where you came from? We belong here—you don't!"

Watching the theatre of this debate, hearing their loud, brittle voices,
each of us seen from the wings by our dim reflections.

READING

And the trams grind around the nearby corner
like the sub-aural thunder
of molars in a stressed jaw,
and the sparrow flits on the roof opposite my window,
watching my blue eyes as they follow
the line of an imperial poet's thought,
those words marching across the page and my tongue
hesitates—

TO OTHER AFRICANS

My brothers, my bluntly fraternal greetings
— as Sengor once wrote to Césaire —
and I will call you my continental brothers
while knowing that each of us is far from home
and that I'm also addressing our sisters,
knowing that in the Australian streets you ignore me,
your eyes downcast as you stroll in your galabias
to evening prayers at the Albanian mosque,
or you stare away off into the distance
as if at a wobbly Paradise

    though I speak in the black tongues of angels and men
I am not invisible

    And I see you all, my African brothers and sisters
—even in absentia—
whether behind the Tuareg-blue tent of a burka
or under a peaked cap GOREE as sunset,
or there on the housing estate's basketball court
intensely pummelling the ground and I hear you when
the mental white poor pace their anger in rap,
when they are reborn as poets—black—
and in the turntablist's phrasing,
the talking/drumming of an old vinyl record

    though I speak in the black tongues of angels and men
I am not invisible

I am not a phantom, albino terrorist, tokeloshe
under your child's bed

Yes, my brothers and sisters...

THE COCKATOO

Others might have expected conversation. We didn't.
Standing with a Malaysian-Chinese man outside his furniture store
on Sydney Road, Brunswick, we have no need to talk.
The Lebanese bloke on his silver bicycle, taking a break from the kebab shop,
glides past us. We don't notice. We don't look up
from the sulphur-crested cockatoo unsteadily perched on the back of a chair.
We are waiting for him to hold forth on the subject of AUSTRALIA.

THE ALGERIAN

— for 'i Professori'

"If you see me wandering the leafy streets of Carlton
in the company of a small Algerian man
with dark glasses and a false nose,
you can rest assured he definitely isn't
Monsieur Jacques Derrida."

THE BANQUET OF CLEOPATRA

— a painting by Giovanni Battista Tiepolo

Her arm is outstretched, its horizontality stilling the feasting, the palace.

Everyone watches her. The wager—
    To host the most expensive banquet in The Known World.

Cleopatra, the African Queen, in extravagant Venetian dress,
                                       is off to the left in the picture,
the miracle of those fluted columns and busy servants
                                        another airy frame around her.

Her hair is bound up, isn't black. She isn't dark-skinned, is unAfrican.

Rigid with competitive arrogance, her arm is silencing us all with a held moment.

Not everyone is watching her. Some have turned away.
Behind her—almost her shadow—the Nubian: *What's he thinking*

as he clears away the plates? Of his lost Saharan village, of his stolen family?

The Roman General, his eyes, though invisible to us, are on her: *Gorgeous.*
And at her fingertips the famous pearl gleaming
                                  like our star seen from another solar system.

Beneath, the goblet of vinegar waits swirling like a blackhole.

Unknown to the Queen, the General and everyone else there,
we of the Southern Hemisphere, beneath the Equator of her arm,

will wait for that precious pearl to fall, slowly, slowly, for that pearl to refuse gravity.

DANGER AQUA PROFUNDA

Exquisite. *She is.* In other argots 'a honey', 'a trophy-wife'.

But here, with all the singles on the sundeck at Fitzroy Pool,
lionised by her sequin-trimmed bikini and her apparent un-self-consciousness,
deified by the previous century's billboards advertising BEAUTY,
this woman, tanned, finely muscled, is poised, like Chaos in a bonsai.

No one is noticing her. I am not even thinking these thoughts.

Her partner, thick-set as a CEO and also bronzed, is unmoved
while she kneels, her spine arched, tossing back her long black hair,
and is also unmoved when she lies back beside him, then slowly
pivots to stroke his thigh with her naked foot,
her toe-ring glittering in the hot, walled-in day, explicit as…

When they are rubbing shoulders—matching tattoos—
behind sunglasses all our eyes are again on them, their animal dominance.

ONE YEAR

In the summer when every terrace house seemed to welcome escaped refugees,
while the War Against Terror was being fought in my name
in the mountains of Afganistan,

I wandered the night streets under the eyes
of quartz-white Anzacs and invisible neurotic possums,
I haunted the suburbs, driving though industrial estates,
waiting inside 24-hour supermarkets

for the voice in my head to cease prattling in Afrikaans,
for me to stop being a luftmensch
and start being a citizen unafraid of the silence that sews twitching lips shut.

Nightly the police helicopter flew overhead,
its spotlight hunting car thieves not asylum seekers,
while in my flat I watched the vase of yellow tulips,
their Dutch clarity unmaking this age

—*We are as permanent as the Statues of Bamiyan until they were exploded;*
We, the frantic, are still in Manhattan's flaming, collapsing Twin Towers,
deciding whether to run down the stairs or up.

In the autumn, when the elms refused to shed their leaves
and I spent the long calm days lounging at the pool,
I found myself explaining nightly to my students that simply being awake
is not insomnia: "It's political."

INVISIBLE CITIES
— for Domenico de Clario

And when you remember where else you have been in your other lives,

being here will be like having sleepily boarded a European ship at noon
to wake startled at midnight on an unimaginable continent in a deserted industrial ci

And you will transform that city into a dreamscape by walking these streets at nig
every leaf sparkling in the avenues of stilled elms
                                    will become a question from another, invisible wo

And being here will be like sitting at an electrical piano,
                                    hearing the murmuring of your fingers,
like transferring all your possessions to some other room,
                                    then taking the floor as your b

or like painting a nocturne blindfolded, the cityscape being in that darkness

as much noise as memory, seeming as Italianate
                                    as those paperbarks in the summer moonli

WEEKEND AWAY

— for S.

After I knelt down between your spreading legs
and told you to watch us in the wardrobe mirror,

and before we lay exhausted on the dishevelled bed
distantly witnessing the lightning-storm blitz across Port Phillip Bay,

we were nothing like the shipwreck of metaphor,
nothing sensational as narcotics or Emptiness.

We were the word—*purified*—that we could later breathe
into our Other's ear.

TERRA NULLIUS

Being interstate I AM the Treeless Plain,
a transit zone, that door through which the world walks
while squinting at the schizoid horizon.

AFTER RETURNING

Walking down the path, dense bush on both sides,
I'm disappointed the wildflowers have already wilted—

native wisteria, yellow starbursts of prickly Moses,
the Azanian gladioli, scarlet kangaroo-paw all gone,

even those negative flowers I can't name or picture now.
Seasons flood through. Whether horizontally or vertically,

whether like aeons gently layered in tiger-striped rock or
speeding like a spray of photographed bullets, who

can say? In my dark mind the succession of blossoming
is like the flicking of the switch for metropolitan lights,

black and forth, click and *Let there be* ...

FERALS

The Local

In these suburbs, what
my yuppie friend called 'The Golden Triangle',
between river and sea, where
professional men and genetically-chosen women,
or vice versa, sleep through this musky briny night,
where the hospital rises
between you and the river like a titanic ocean liner,
the river where prawners
up to their necks in black water trawl wide nets past
laughing sharks and unsmiling dolphins,
in these suburbs there're huge seditious roaches
immigrant and native birds,
possums and even, like me, foxes
—expert survivalists cosmopolitan as you like—
who hide in the parkland and limestone
caves on the foreshore, who mesmerise chooks in the
millionaire's backyard and are never
sighted slinking down these leafy streets.

Those Immigrants

See those rainbow lorikeets
crisscrossing the sky quick-as-a-wink?
they're second or third generation
Queensland immigrants. Now they
behave like locals: they're up at Middle
Swan in the morning, feasting
in the orchards; over Kings Park and
my head in the arvo; and, at
this time of year, this evening
they'll be down at Cottesloe
in the Norfolk pines, roaring
like a bushfire-sunset
but invisible to us.

OUT THERE

Fields of purple toxin behind
fences glinting like threads of spun-out
webs flanked the road leading us through
the country town. As we drove through,
over the bridge, following the railway tracks,
I spoke about 'our laureate' and about that mother
who, in her weatherboard, sells phone-sex.
When we arrived the house was an old hotel,
a watering-hole in the middle of twilight plains.
When we arrived the gay couple shook our hands,
the hetero couple ("A Pom and a Victorian!")
sat down with us for dinner, introducing
us to the man in flannel shirt and ug boots who'd
worked in every desert, on oil rigs, and could speak
fluent Arabic. We have arrived when he tells us
jokes about the 'Abos', and that next year he would be
defusing landmines for anyone who'd pay him well enough.

NYOONGAR COUNTRY

The Statue of Mokare

I'm walking down the colony's main street
when I sight the statue outside the Shire office.

And when I approach the bronze—*It's Mokare,*
the native whose past was Co-Existence, a cordial greeting.

Two kids are hanging from his arms, kicking his shins,
while their crouching nanna chatters: "I'm keeping a beady eye on them."

Noticing that I'm reading the plaque, she calls out again, amiable,
though I can't understand her. She points at the kids, cackling,

telling them off. I'm not a local: *My plaque would be an apologia.*
For some time I stand there wondering what to say.

The Novelist's Comments

After I read my poem addressed to one of his people's heroes,
in his reclaimed, autochthonous voice
the novelist doesn't say:

> *This is our language, our land.*

Nor does he say:

> *Why don't you go back where you came from?*

And in what he doesn't say he is echoing the woman
who after burying her father—a rare fluent speaker of language—
declared she should have chucked his tapes and journals,
his repository of the tongue, after him into the mouth
of the grave:

> *So that the white bastards wouldn't get that too.*

GIRRAWEEN LIBRARY

The yellow bible-thick book of Aboriginal Sign Language is open
on my lap and I'm silenced, imprinted by the
afterglow of the dingy library, by my reading there are times
when not to speak: *As when after someone's*
died, when the voice can distract, anger the spirit:
Hand signals then. Then
I heard the breeze—in my cannot-speak—like
the calm spontaneous gust in Tarkovski's *Mirror*
pressing grass down.
Pneuma.

DURING THE HEATWAVE

Desert wind's been blowing for the past week
so I stay in the unit, drape bedsheets over the hot glass
of the windows. Our plants wilt, even while I drain bottles of water
into their parched mouths. In the semi-darkness I
sit at my trestle table or on the mattress in the other room.
Dreams of the Pilbara dissolve into reveries
of my sprouting wings, gliding over familiar Crown Land.
Like the anecdote of the blackfella who was 'given'
a postcard-sized board and told to re-paint the large-as-life croc
("HE ONLY PAINTED ONE FOOT!"), I'm invisibly edged.
To me now any sentence is a road into rippling magnesium flame,
and my skinless body-mind is only seen in this darkened room
that's detaching from the ground.

PLACES OF REFUGE

Up in the Hills

Hidden away up in the hills, off a gravel road through an abandoned orchard,
there is a place alive in my mind, a notional country

of white-skinned wandoo and grasstrees and granite outcrops.

There the bull-ants are monstrous, magnified by quiet,
and the stilled kangaroos are hesitant self-portraits.

There, once, with the evening breeze rising up from the valley
stirring the she-oaks, too slight to wake the other trees, I,

like this glade, this breathing-space, this land, became: untouched:

psyche.

The Serpentine Monastery

Having stood in line and offered my spoonful of rice to each of the monks,
then watched the middle-aged Thai women bow to them,

I recall how, by accident, I'd found my friend's hut on the burnt-out hillside
and had foreseen him telling me that the Buddha had taught non-proliferation.

This place, slippery as the ball-bearing gravel,
.................................impersonal as the parrotbush and contorted banksias,

is both a refuge from the new economies and from what I will call THE SNAKE.

THE PLACE

(—we, washed up
here, like the whale
beached and chopped
into manageable, truck-sized
chunks and secretly buried
to be later exhumed,
to become bones in a museum—we,
like the lost leopard seal,
head rock-smooth as a philosopher's,
long mouth like an untamed
dog's, we snarl and slap,
out of our element, as
if limbless, as if we understood
our role yet remained
autistic—like the Dutch explorers,
finding this beach under
their boat, the backwash like
a crowd of withdrawing snakes, we
struggle on solid sand, through
alienating bush, and capture
black swans of which, one
historian will say, the
Romans already knew—)

nothing but a
foreign breeze...

MEMORIALS

Watching the football

Up here, high 'in the wings', our gaze is godly,
        triple: of the monitors bolted to the rafters,
of the monster-screen on the far side of the stadium,
        and of the players down there, miniscule warriors
on a green field, an oval, one surface

        inside our cone of vision. Sporting, the teams;
their players' names shouted through these spectators' mouths,
        the children and adults all barracking
in a world inhuman, after The Person, mental
        with flag-waving, chanting and the pretence that we are

all here. The group beside me is an ironic soundtrack,
        their commentary local, dinkum,
like our beer's watery bitterness, and we postpone our own regally absent
        voices. While down there the intelligent ball
—the oval's tiny heart—has no idea of the trajectory of its mood-swings.

Landmarks

The daemon I am is descending the stairs
    in a heritage hotel in The Rocks,
his every atom nude, shuddering slightly,
    each step made cautiously,
while behind, high over the rooftops,
    the flung ventriloquist's arc of the Harbour Bridge,
and across the ferry-churned night
    the Opera House is a cinematic flickering.

Pre-empting my being that daemon
    seated before landscapes in the Museum of Contemporary Art,
observing the bush differentiating into Greek geometries,
    an empty, luminous cursive becoming a scribbling,
I'm dreaming that blindness
    as my own evaporating Braille,
as those caresses that won't wake the sleeper
    but will comfort him.

Look. Look, I encourage my daemon.
    Your eyes are the way through
before the mouth forms a gateway of air.
    Yes, look, I am whispering while gliding down the skew stairs
of a hotel that has no other logic
    than the shore's edge
and that Papunya-style dot-dot-dot
    of the Harbour's deepwater voice.

~

An ocular whipping, this severe scalding Westralian summer light
that beats us from the brightness of the circular gaol courtyard,
from beneath the prying commander's upstairs window

and into one of those shadowy cells that gets under your skin
and grips you; the closed gnawed-at door keeping you from your memory,
the stillness graffitiing your soul's outline on the wall's raw limestone.

Here above the burning ocean on this modest pitted cliff under strange flags,
you are in the hold of a convict ship run aground
with the tide falling. But admitting this as abandonment,

you are also a vortex of other memories, despite the cell's monastic comforts,
its briny chill and its immediacy that, like the scent

of native peppermint leaves crushed in the hand,
inhaled to clear the mind, is a blind bush-medicine.

~

Ruins in the field of vision, eroded
beacons, menhirs or foundations exposed in the glowing white sand,

this outcropping blade- and shadow-sharp, an affluent dayblindness;
everywhere shiny falling coins.

Deep in the eyes' dim cavities, the presence of sweeping Aeolian sand
is a voice, a blackness—

The columns, rocky and pocked, once the roots of invisible trees,
now fangs in a tongueless mouth—

     From here in this windshadow, behind the sedge-hairy dunes,
the Pinnacles Desert is

that tiny thorny-devil lizard stretched out flat before first light,
its back a spiny landscape of peaks and ravines

which coax the dewdrop
to walk into its mouth.

Masks

Each mask has its own cabinet, as an exhibited slave would,
and its own plinth tall and schematic as an emptied coffin.

But a deathmask is not an image: it's a face pressed up against darkness,
into the material where a poet and bushranger, an admiral and a murderer
are equally solid, equally moonlight and fingerprints on shattered, evidential glass.

These dead faces, neither calling out for Oblivion
nor warning away Eternity's perpetually absent weather,
are John Dodo's spirit-doctor, Marparn,
                              proliferating in his police line-up of stone heads

and that avenue of vandalised and stolen and indefatigably returning
prime ministerial bronzes I once saw in a town quiet since the Gold Rush.

                              ~

Assailed by 'the natives', those plants

                          cultivated as evidence of wealth prior to Invasion,
by their luminescence, their harsh insistence as of a persistent after-image,
a spotfire crackling in a retinal forest, accosted by the relics of botanical glory,

I see above me on the slope, my back to the Swan River and the Brewery Site
down there, Africa far to the west, that I am a comrade of these exiles,

these Gondwanaland trees that seem, transplanted in their orange gravel,
like giant beer bottles presenting us with shrivelled desiccated flowers,
these boabs, baobabs, that are—another insistence—*novelistic*:

       a prolix haven wherein the escaped slave must hide
despite the distractions of passing animals and the trinkets
                         left by her worshipping bushmen

The Captive

Akin to the wombat-hole in which the woman hid to escape her rapists
and to the refuge that The Church was before this age of disembodied war,

the ex-dictator's stony face is a mountain of caves,
his eyes, ears and mouth are all being inspected for subversives

by the disinterested army doctor with his torch and spatula
who no doubt in the future will brag of this moment of capitulation

that on my TV screen here in this far-flung province of the Empire of the Obvious
is not the event of displaying a face,

but the affirmation that the defeated man is actually

you.

THE DIWAN

New Year's Eve

Behind the white gables of Perth Mosque,
around the corner from the block of flats where she used to live,

she who held my heart in her hands like an injured bird,
whose laugh tinkled like a meditation bell waking me,

down a narrow street of old workers' cottages, in a friend's backyard
a bearded man, whose eyes are Sumerian,

whose deep voice is calm and burning like Zoroastrian fire,
recites a classical Persian poem:

> *When I am drunk I wander down the street*
> *unaware that I am passing the house of my beloved.*

Then the poem modernised:

> *I'm so drunk when I wander down the street of my beloved*
> *that only when I am pissing against the wall I realise it's hers.*

O were I drunk enough to lean against my ex-beloved's door
having nothing in mind but the words of an Iranian's poem!

Elegy

As soon as the lifeguards are off duty,
a dark, invisible hand is pulling him through the curtains of his memory.

Then his parents—not weeping—are calling out his name,
scanning the swimmers in the Cottesloe swell to see

the young man who isn't there, who last week had told
how he was already elsewhere, within earshot of Allah, and free.

And they are asking: *What is love if you can't find your baby?*
What is a voice, if his face is turned away permanently?

Nothing but a foreign breeze, hot, easterly,
flipping through the blank book of waves, searching for his name?

ACKNOWLEDGEMENTS

The poems in this book have previously appeared, sometimes in a different form, in the following publications:

newspapers: *The Age, The Australian, The West Australian*

journals: *Atlanta Review, Antipodes, Cordite, Heat, Imago, Island, Manoa, Meanjin, Nethra, Overland, Salt, Southern Hemisphere Review, Southerly, Westerly*

online: *c-side, How2connect, Thylazine, Western Australian Writing*

anthologies: *Calyx: Thirty Contemporary Australian Poets* (Paper Bark Press), *New Music* (Five Islands Press), *Ngara: Living in this Place Now* (Five Islands Press)

pamphlets: *The Civic Poems* (SC Editions) and *The Brewery Site* (Rare Objects Series, No. 37, Vagabond Press)

And in the book-length collections: *Burning Swans, Anachronism, Barefoot Speech, Loanwords* and *The Ancient Capital of Images* (all Fremantle Arts Centre Press)

BOOKS BY JOHN MATEER

FREMANTLE PRESS
Burning Swans
Anachronism
Barefoot Speech
Loanwords
Semar's Cave: an Indonesian Journal
The Ancient Capital of Images

SALT, UK
Elsewhere

SISYPHUS, AUSTRIA
Ex-White (in translation)

TEA FOR ONE, PORTUGAL
Namban (in translation, forthcoming)

HUACANAMO, SPAIN
Ex-White (in translation, forthcoming)

John Mateer *SEMAR'S CAVE. An Indonesian Journal*

In the Australian mind, no nation poses a bigger cultural impasse than Indonesia. Is there ever a possibility of real cultural exchange?

At the heart of John Mateer's journal is this very disturbing question: Why do we travel? Must cultural transactions remain substantially economic and exploitative? Do we only seek what we think we already know?

Mateer brings a poetic integrity and a gentle calm to his detailed representations of daily life in Indonesia. The shock of the foreign is in many ways only the surface layer of the fears and fascinations we assume. More deeply embedded is the notion that we never really understand ourselves until we become foreign. With that as his ethical focus, John Mateer has succeeded where so many others have failed, by revealing the complex and dangerous liaisons between individual history and mass nationalism.—*Brian Castro*

FREMANTLE
fine independent publishing **PRESS**

Published 2010
FREMANTLE PRESS
25 Quarry Street, Fremantle
(PO Box 158, North Fremantle, 6159)
Western Australia
www.fremantlepress.com.au

Consultant editors Wendy Jenkins/Georgia Richter
Typeset by furrylogic.com.au
Cover design Ally Crimp
Cover image Mike Gray, 'Eden Caprice 2009'

A catalogue record for this
book is available from the
NATIONAL
LIBRARY   National Library of Australia
OF AUSTRALIA

ISBN 9781921361869

Fremantle Press is supported by the Western Australian
State Government through the Department of Cultural
Industries, Tourism and Sport.

Fremantle Press respectfully acknowledges the Whadjuk people of
the Noongar nation as the Traditional Owners and Custodians of
the land where we work in Walyalup